Advance Praise
Late-Night Phone Calls

"Weird title alert: what do an insect, a condiment, and something by definition considered an inconvenience have to do with each other? And how did they come together to form a book title? It would be better for Daphne Tarango to explain that—as she does well in the introduction to her book. Suffice it to say she has found that each of them adds uniquely to her life and, more importantly, she has remembered to thank God for them. Not just in a whispered thank you as she falls asleep but in a committed several-times-daily journaling that helps her not to forget what God has done for her."

—**Vicki Huffman**, *Freelance Editor and Author*

"If you're a novice at journaling or you've been doing it for years . . . you will be blessed by *Dragonflies, Ketchup, and Late-Night Phone Calls*. This title drew me in immediately, and Daphne's beautiful way of sharing each story is just as engaging. She has the ability to look beyond her circumstances to the blessing. If you're anything like me, you need this book."

—**Deb Wolf**, *Managing Editor at Five Minutes for Faith and author of Sarah's Garden, a modern-day parable for girls of all ages*

"In this unique thankfulness journal, Daphne Tarango shares her struggles openly and honestly, and by humble example, inspires us with what the Lord Jesus Christ has done and is doing through her life. You will enjoy Daphne's encouragement to record your own daily blessings from God in your life."

—**Beth Willis Miller**, *M.Ed., member of AWSA, Advanced Writers and Speakers Association*

"There are several positive aspects to this wonderful journal of thanksgiving. The Lord has used Daphne to create a journaling, worship experience for almost any age from older children to adults. As I read the Scriptures and Daphne's comments, it brings my soul to a place of peace that allows me to see all our Lord has done for us, which in turn, brings thankfulness into my life instead of the busy pressures of this world. I would definitely recommend *Dragonflies, Ketchup, and Late-Night Phone Calls* to everyone. I'm sure it is a book that I will use over and over to guide me to be truly thankful to my Lord for all He has done. I am personally thankful to my Lord and to Daphne for this fine book.

—**Jerry Goodell**, *Sr. Associate Pastor of Pastoral Care, First Baptist Church at the Mall, Lakeland, Florida*

31 Days of Journaling God's Blessings

DRAGONFLIES, *Ketchup* & LATE-NIGHT *Phone Calls*

DAPHNE TARANGO

Dragonflies, Ketchup, and Late-Night Phone Calls:

31 Days of Journaling God's Blessings

Daphne E. Tarango
DaphneWrites – Comfort for the Journey
Comfort Station Publications
Lakeland, Florida, USA
daphnetarango@gmail.com

Dragonflies, Ketchup, and Late-Night Phone Calls: 31 Days of Journaling God's Blessings
Copyright © 2013 Daphne E. Tarango
Comfort Station Publications
Lakeland, Florida, USA
ISBN-13: 978-0615926551
Printed by CreateSpace, An Amazon.com Company
Available from Amazon.com, CreateSpace.com, and other retail outlets

Front and back cover photography and design Copyright © 2013 Garcia Photography.

Back cover head shot of Daphne Tarango Copyright © 2013 Sarah L. Farnsworth.

All rights reserved. No portion of this book may be used or reproduced by any means, graphic, electronic, mechanical, including photocopying, recording, taping, or by any information storage retrieval system without the written permission of the author except in the case of brief quotations embodied in articles and reviews.

Scripture quotations marked (NIV) are taken from the Holy Bible, New International Version®, NIV®. Copyright © 1973, 1978, 1984, 2011 by Biblica, Inc.™ Used by permission of Zondervan. All rights reserved worldwide. www.zondervan.com The "NIV" and "New International Version" are trademarks registered in the United States Patent and Trademark Office by Biblica, Inc.™

Scripture quotations marked (NIrV) are taken from the Holy Bible, New International Reader's Version®, NIrV® Copyright © 1995, 1996, 1998 by Biblica, Inc.™ Used by permission of Zondervan. All rights reserved worldwide. www.zondervan.com The "NIrV" and "New International Reader's Version" are trademarks registered in the United States Patent and Trademark Office by Biblica, Inc.™

Dedication

I dedicate this book to my Lord and Savior,

Jesus Christ,

and to my family,

for whom I have much to be thankful.

Table of Contents

Acknowledgments iii
Introduction v
How To Use This Book xi
Day 1 1
Day 2 5
Day 3 9
Day 4 13
Day 5 17
Day 6 21
Day 7 25
Day 8 29
Day 9 33
Day 10 37
Day 11 41
Day 12 45
Day 13 49
Day 14 53
Day 15 57
Day 16 61
Day 17 65
Day 18 69
Day 19 73
Day 20 77

Day 21 81
Day 22..85
Day 23 89
Day 24..93
Day 25 97
Day 26 101
Day 27 105
Day 28..109
Day 29 113
Day 30 117
Day 31 121
Thank You..125
List of Bible Verses Used 127
List of Quotes Used...135
About Daphne..145
Connect with Daphne 147

Acknowledgments

I am indebted to the many people who encourage, motivate, and support me in my writing efforts.

To my writing group: Thank you for your feedback at our monthly meetings in person, online, and via telephone. Your quick turnaround time for feedback has helped me to improve on the concept and title of this book.

To my advance reviewers: Thank you for your time invested in reading and providing feedback. Your honesty helped me to continue in this work. Thank you for encouraging me.

To Garcia Photography: Thank you for the lovely cover photo and design. You captured my vision for this book and ran with it. May God continue to bless your talents and your business.

To my husband: You have encouraged me from the moment you knew I wanted to write. You are my cheerleader, even when I struggle cheering myself on. You take care of things around the house when I am "in the zone." And you father—and mother—our children when I need to get my thoughts and feelings on paper, on computer, or on my voice recorder. What a gift you are to me! I love you.

To my children: Thank you for being patient with me when I spend a lot of time at the computer. I thank

God He brought us together almost two years ago. You have given me plenty to thank God for. I love you.

To my parents: Thank you for believing in me and for the times you smile with pride when I show you what I'm working on. Thank you for your "Right on, girl!" or "That's my girl!" and for your "Ayyy, Babyyy!" You've never given up on me, even when I was making bad choices. Thank you for praying for me even now.

To my dear friend Terry: Thank you for reminding me to thank God for three things every night—and for writing them down. Your faithfulness in journaling God's blessings was an inspiration for this book.

To a long-ago friend Deana: Thank you for the many years you placed three kernels of corn on our plates before Thanksgiving dinners and had everyone around the table give thanks for three things in their lives. You set this all in motion.

Introduction

Dragonflies fascinate me. Iridescent colors drape their bodies in shades I've never seen. They flutter around in loops, forward, and yes, even backward. They perch on car antennas, still water, delicate blades of grass, or any place they can stop and rest for a few moments. I've heard they even land on people sometimes. (That hasn't happened to me yet, although I'm hopeful.) Before you know it, dragonflies shoot up into the air pirouetting around everything and anything with freedom in their wings. I imagine them laughing with delight as they spin and twirl. Then, they're off—just as quickly as they appeared.

They tend to find me—dragonflies. And it's usually when I've most needed encouragement: After a long day at work. Trying to corral my kids in the grocery store parking lot. Sitting in the carport after a long afternoon of helping with homework. It's as if God sends me messengers of cheer to remind me of His presence and His comfort. His hugs. His caress.

Whenever a dragonfly zips into view, my lips curl upward into a smile; I just can't help it. On several occasions, I've had not one, not two, but three dragonflies dancing around me. Pure delight!

On those days, I thank God for dragonflies.

Ketchup doesn't fascinate me like dragonflies do. Ketchup humbles me. Whenever I set the table for dinner, and someone—usually the children—asks for ketchup, I remember serving dinner on a rainy Saturday evening at Talbot House Ministries several years ago.

I stretched my hair net over my curls, washed my hands, and put on gloves. As I walked to the serving station, my eyes scanned the room. Raining and storming outside. A couple hundred people inside. Young. Old. Black. White. Down on their luck. Homeless.

A booming voice emerged out of the crowd, "Let us pray." I bowed my head and listened. In my heart, I prayed, "Lord, please multiply this food."

And so it began. Burgers. Fries. Bread. Lettuce. Sweet tea. And ice cream. I had the lettuce. It was last on the food line, which gave me the honor of handing each person their plate and asking how each person was doing. I could smile, look them in the eyes, and joke with them about eating their veggies.

Someone on my team set out the condiments: Ketchup, mustard, mayonnaise, and all the burger fixings. A middle-aged woman—not more than 5-feet tall—picked up her plate, turned around toward the tables, and stopped.

"Ketchup and mustard?!?! That's rich people stuff."

She rushed over and piled the condiments onto her plate like a child let loose in a candy store.

Every time I put ketchup on my table—whether we're having a feast or a bowl of spaghetti noodles and beans, I remember: I am indeed wealthy.

On those days, I thank God for ketchup.

I usually don't thank God for late-night phone calls, but lately they have been very much welcome in my home.

My husband has been laid-off for six weeks and unable to find work locally. We have done everything we know to do so he won't have to find industrial construction work out of town, but as with many others in this economy, the phone calls don't come and the emails seem to go unanswered even after sending out countless applications and résumés.

The past couple months have been incredibly difficult for us financially, emotionally, and yes, even spiritually. My husband hasn't wanted to go out of town. I haven't wanted him to go out of town. And our three children whom we adopted mid-last year haven't wanted him to go out of town either. After dwindling resources, we had to make that difficult decision. As I write this, he has been away almost four weeks.

It's hard to be positive on days when the kids are acting up; I have a neck ache, backache, anything-ache. Even dinnertime becomes a madhouse. On that first night my husband was out of town, my body sank into my queen-size foam mattress. I gravitated toward his side of the bed and drifted off to sleep. The phone rang, but my eyes and my mind shrugged off the noise. As it continued to ring, my eyes stood at attention fearing something was wrong with a loved one.

"Hello?"

There it was: My husband's voice.

"Hi, honey."

It was like our dating days—all lovey-dovey.

"No, you hang up."

"No, you hang up."

When we were dating, we started a tradition of telling each other our favorite and least favorite things of the day. It really helped us to stay connected hundreds of miles away. These past few weeks, we've continued our tradition, just as we did when we were dating and even as we do when we're together.

Yes, I look forward to—and even thank God for—late-night phone calls.

***

It's easy to complain when things aren't going as I would like. Even on good days, I find myself complaining more than thanking God for his love and goodness.

Yes, I thank God for the "big" things: Family, friends, food, shelter, church. But when I'm going through a difficult time, I can't seem to recall the concrete ways God has blessed me in the past: A dragonfly on a stressful day. The last squirts of ketchup on some French fries. Those late-night phone calls from my husband when he's working out of town.

This is why I wrote this journal: To jot down other specific blessings from God and for *you* to jot down your own dragonfly, ketchup, and late-night phone-call blessings. When you use *Dragonflies, Ketchup, and Late-Night Phone Calls,* you'll be able to look back and see how

God blew you a kiss, caressed your face, and whispered, "I. Love. You."

On good days, bad days, or difficult seasons, *Dragonflies, Ketchup, and Late-Night Phone Calls* can help you find even one thing for which to thank God. That one thing can make your day brighter, your night more peaceful, and your life more enjoyable.

Ready?

How To Use This Book

So how do you use *Dragonflies, Ketchup, and Late-Night Phone Calls?*

Each of the 31 days in this blessings journal begins with a biblical verse about thankfulness. This opening verse sets the stage for a general prayer of praise and thanksgiving for that day. I encourage you to read the verse and the prayer, to use it during your quiet times at morning or night, or to meditate on it throughout the day. If something in the prayer resonates with you, I encourage you to write it on the notes page at the end of each day.

Dragonflies, Ketchup, and Late-Night Phone Calls is unique in that it goes beyond general thank-yous to God. After the opening prayer, you will see a page on which you can quickly fill in your specific blessings for that day. Remember, you can use the notes page at the end of each chapter for jotting down more thank-yous to God.

At first, it might be difficult to remember specific blessings on any given day. But I've designed *Dragonflies, Ketchup, and Late-Night Phone Calls* to help you along the way. Each day has four sections: Morning, mid-day, evening, and bedtime.

- The **morning section** can be used to thank God for something that happened early in the day or to tell God what you're looking forward to that day. If there isn't anything in particular you're looking forward to, feel free to mention what you're worried about and to thank God for some aspect of that request. For example, if you're worried about a meeting and presentation at work that day, you could say, "Father, I'm worried about this meeting, and I'm not sure it will go well. But thank you that they chose me to speak. Thank you that they believe in me and trust I will do a great job. Amen." This section is great to start your day with a lens of thankfulness.

- The **mid-day section** can be used to thank God for specifics that occurred from morning to the middle of your day—be it lunch, breaks between classes, children's nap times, etc. Again, the key is to focus on something specific. For example, if the meeting you were nervous about went well, thank God for it. If you usually have a difficult time getting your toddler to eat her food, and on that day, she ate it without a fuss, you could say, "Thank you God for little Mary eating all her food without throwing it at me or at the dog."
- The **evening section** is set aside for journaling how God has blessed you from mid-day to say, dinnertime, the end of your workday, when you pick up the kids from school, when you're done with your college classes, etc. For example, if you rarely make it to the gym after work but you did on that day, you could say, "Thank you, God, for making a way for me to work out at the gym today."
- The **bedtime** section is for anything that occurred from the evening to the time you lie down for the night. This could be a few extra minutes to watch television, a quiet time to read or relax. Or if you

remember—which I suspect you will—other things that happened throughout the day, then jot them down too.

I've purposely labeled each section with these headings and not written, for example, "This morning, I am thankful for...." I believe it is important for you—and for me—to write out, "Thank you God for..." It reminds us from whom all blessings flow.

After each section, you will see the words: "For these things, I thank you. Amen." As I mentioned earlier, I envision each journal entry as its own prayer of praise and thanksgiving. This sentence brings the prayer together with one final thanks and affirmation.

At the end of each day, you will see a quote on thankfulness. Feel free to use the notes section at the end of each day to write about the quote as well.

My hope is that you will carry *Dragonflies, Ketchup, and Late-Night Phone Calls* with you throughout the day and jot down the blessings as you experience them. Doing so will lift your spirits and remind you how God is with you every minute of the day. I guarantee: You *will* see more and more of his goodness in your life. You *will* want to write it down!

At the end of the 31 days, you will have one big praise report of God's goodness. You can use it to encourage yourself, to inspire others, or both. You can use it to share your testimony with others: Family, friends, grandchildren, even strangers.

Dragonflies, Ketchup, and Late-Night Phone Calls is great for young and old, men and women, people going through difficult seasons. It can even be used with a group: Each person can share how God has blessed them each day.

Dragonflies, Ketchup, and Late-Night Phone Calls can be used by people facing specific issues and circumstances. People with chronic illnesses can use it to jot down small blessings that remind them of God's strength when they have little to none. Also, people in recovery can use *Dragonflies, Ketchup, and Late-Night Phone Calls* to document small victories on their recovery journeys. It also makes a great gift.

Dragonflies, Ketchup, and Late-Night Phone Calls may just become your ongoing journal. Once you're finished with the 31 days, you can start again with a fresh copy. What a great legacy of thanksgiving!

One final note: If you're unable—or forget—to write down your blessings throughout the day, the journal is still a great way to reflect on God's blessings before going to sleep. Remember, you don't have to be rigid.

Have fun with it!

*"They stood every morning to thank and praise the Lord.
They did the same thing every evening."*

1 Chronicles 23:30 NIrV

Day 1

"Give thanks no matter what happens. God wants you to thank him because you believe in Christ Jesus."

1 Thessalonians 5:18, NIrV

No matter what, God!

I will come to you and thank you. I wasn't able to approach you—the holy God. But Jesus washed me clean. White as snow! Now I can stand before you to thank you myself. Thank you!

I believe in Jesus and because I believe in him and who he says he is—son of the living God, I thank you. Because I believe in what he says he'll do, I thank you. You will come through. You do not lie. I can count on you.

Thank you for Jesus' example of giving thanks in all situations and in all circumstances. Thank you that I can lift my eyes to you in times of need; I know you hear me. Thank you for not turning your head. Thank you for working things out in my life. I don't need to worry.

As you were with Jesus, I know you are forever with me—good or bad. If the sun shines on me today, I will praise you. If dark clouds transform blue skies into gray, I will still sing praises to your name.

In all things, I will be intentional about giving you thanks. I will purpose in my heart to acknowledge you at all times. I will give you thanks—no matter what.

Morning Thank You:

Mid-Day Thank You:

Evening Thank You:

Bedtime Thank You:

For these things, I thank you. Amen.

Notes for Day 1

"Perhaps it takes a purer faith to praise God for unrealized blessings than for those we once enjoyed or those we enjoy now."

A.W. Tozer

Day 2

"Give thanks to the Lord, because he is good. His faithful love continues forever."

Psalm 107:1, NIrV

You are good, Father!

When I wake, your love greets me with a kiss. Thank you.

Everything you do is good. Everything you want for me is good. You are good! Nothing can shake your goodness and love for me.

Your goodness always benefits me, Father; I choose to believe it. Even when life is pungent, you release the aroma of your goodness and remind me you are good. Thank you.

I am forever secure in your love, my Lord. No worries, no reason to fear. You are devoted to me; you are near. Jesus: Faithful, loyal master. My Lord, I cling to you. I clasp my hand in yours. United. Together. Married forever.

Things of this world come and go, but you are eternal, O God. Family and friends enter and leave this world; you are still with me. Thank you. Careers begin and end, but you, O Lord, are my pursuit. Health wanes, but with you, I am whole.

I thank you.

Morning Thank You:

Mid-Day Thank You:

Evening Thank You:

Bedtime Thank You:

For these things, I thank you. Amen.

Notes for Day 2

"We pray for the big things and forget to give thanks for the ordinary, small (and yet really not small) gifts."

Dietrich Bonhoeffer

Day 3

"Thanks be to God for his indescribable gift!"

2 Corinthians 9:15, NIV

You are indescribable, God!

What a gift you are to me! You are the good news to this hurting world—to my world. My heart ached before receiving your gift of Jesus. He healed my pain and soothed my hurts. Thank you.

Jesus is the ultimate gift. Jesus: Praise to your name! Praise to you, beautiful one. Praise to you, rich became poor. Praise to you, gift of the Father, now and forevermore.

You gave the greatest gift, O God, yet you keep giving me more. The greatest gift and lesser, everyday gifts—all from your bounty, your heart, your warehouse, your store. Thank you.

I cannot comprehend the ways you touch my life. But thank you for reaching into my heart and mind, for soothing the restlessness that overtakes me at times. Thank you for slowing down my racing mind and bringing it back to the present. Thank you for the gift of now.

At times, it's hard to see your gifts in my life, God. Sometimes your gifts come disguised. I choose to see beyond the veil of my circumstances and thank you for lifting it in due time.

You are beyond words. You are indescribable!

Morning Thank You:

Mid-Day Thank You:

Evening Thank You:

Bedtime Thank You:

For these things, I thank you. Amen.

Notes for Day 3

"Here are the two best prayers I know: 'Help me, help me, help me' and 'Thank you, thank you, thank you.'"

Anne Lamott

Day 4

"Give thanks to the LORD, call on his name; make known among the nations what he has done."

Psalm 105:1, NIV

Thank you, my Lord!

You gave me a better life—the best life! I will share you with others. I will look for divine meetings with those who need hope. Thank you for bringing the right people into my life. Thank you for the right words at the right time.

I can't do life without you, God. Thank you for taking care of it for me. Thank you for filtering problems through your hands, for safeguarding my mind and my heart.

When trying times come, I cry out to you, and you are there. Thank you for being present, for responding to my call.

Lord, my Lord! I want to bring you fame: How you rise for me, how you come to me and care for me, how you love. Thank you.

I am your missionary—a bearer of good news to my world. Thank you for surrounding me, for covering me, for shielding me from harm.

Your Word triumphs through the ages, Lord. Your story lives forevermore. Thank you for victory. Thank you for wonders. Thank you for miracles. I will share you with others; thank you for trusting me with your Word.

Morning Thank You:

Mid-Day Thank You:

Evening Thank You:

Bedtime Thank You:

For these things, I thank you. Amen.

Notes for Day 4

"There is a way to live the big of giving thanks in all things. It is this: to give thanks in this one small thing. The moments will add up."

Ann Voskamp

Day 5

"Spend a lot of time in prayer. Always be watchful and thankful."

Colossians 4:2, NIrV

I'm on the watch, Lord!

I will keep my eyes open. I will stay alert. I will awake to your hand in my life today. Thank you for spiritual eyes to see you.

Thank you for a heart that senses needs in others and responds in compassion toward them. Thank you for opportunities to pray with others.

Thank you for chiseling hearts of stone into hearts that beat with life. You did it for me, Lord. Thank you! I was lifeless, but you stooped down to embrace me. You revived my heart; thank you.

I will talk to you throughout the day. You are my life-support, the one who gives me breath. I keep you on my mind and in my heart. I set aside my time with you. I know that no time is wasted when it is spent on prayer. I exchange my time to praise and admire your name.

I want to pray without end.

Morning Thank You:

Mid-Day Thank You:

Evening Thank You:

Bedtime Thank You:

For these things, I thank you. Amen.

Notes for Day 5

"A state of mind that sees God in everything is evidence of growth in grace and a thankful heart."

Charles Finney

Day 6

"Do everything you say or do in the name of the Lord Jesus. Always give thanks to God the Father through Christ."

Colossians 3:17, NIrV

One way, my Lord!

    I come to you only through Jesus. In humility, he trekked to the cross. In humility, he hung on the tree. In humility, he breathed his last and gave his life for me. In humility, I thank you.

    Thank you for protecting the name of Jesus in everything I do. I thank you, my God, for controlling my words so they honor you. Thank you for the knowledge that everything I say reflects on your Son. Praise his name!

    Thank you for helping me point others to him—not to me. Not my glory, Lord. Jesus: Yours is the glory.

Thank you that it doesn't take big things to lift Jesus' name. Even the smallest act of kindness can raise his banner for all to see.

Thank you that even seemingly negative situations can be used to point others to Jesus. Thank you that they are opportunities for you to shine brighter in the dark.

Thank you that your light directs my steps. Thank you for being the light that never goes out.

Morning Thank You:

Mid-Day Thank You:

Evening Thank You:

Bedtime Thank You:

For these things, I thank you. Amen.

Notes for Day 6

"God is pleased with no music below so much as with the thanksgiving songs of relieved widows and supported orphans; of rejoicing, comforted, and thankful persons."

Jeremy Taylor

Day 7

"Give thanks as you enter the gates of his temple. Give praise as you enter its courtyards. Give thanks to him and praise his name."

Psalm 100:4, NIrV

My King!

I come to you singing and dancing your praises. I offer you thanks. I offer you my life. I offer you my essence, my soul. Here it is for you.

As I start this day, I want to enter your presence. Thank you that you are near. I don't have to travel to you. You are here!

For opening your doors to me, thank you. For summoning me into your presence, thank you, my Lord. For stretching your hand to me, welcoming me to your throne. Oh, thank you. For lifting me up into your lap, my Daddy, thank you. For hugging me tight, thank you. For loving me, thank you.

I make myself at home in your presence. I drink from your cup of gladness and feast from your plate of peace.

I bless your name. I sing new songs to you—songs of life and love, songs of freedom and joy. None compares to your greatness, my Lord. None can rise higher than you. You are above all. I acknowledge you. I bow to you.

Morning Thank You:

Mid-Day Thank You:

Evening Thank You:

Bedtime Thank You:

For these things, I thank you. Amen.

Notes for Day 7

"Yes, give thanks for 'all things' for, as it has been well said 'Our disappointments are but His appointments.'"

A.W. Pink

Day 8

"You and your families will eat at the place the LORD your God will choose. He will be with you there. You will find joy in everything you have done. That's because he has blessed you."

Deuteronomy 12:7, NIrV

You have blessed me, Lord!

    You have prepared a feast for me. I join you at your table. I feast in your presence, O God.

    You distribute the plates of your pleasures. With joy, you heap spoonfuls of love on me. You quench my thirst. Thank you for giving me of yourself.

    You love my company, Father. You smile when I crave your presence. Thank you for your affection to me. I love being together.

I've found joy with you, God. My heart rests even in times of stress. I know you have the answers, Lord. You are the answer. Thank you.

I enjoy my place in life, Lord. You have set me here. You have positioned me for your purpose: To bring praise to your name.

I celebrate you, my Father. I celebrate your love. I celebrate your salvation. I celebrate Jesus.

You have blessed me, Lord!

Morning Thank You:

Mid-Day Thank You:

Evening Thank You:

Bedtime Thank You:

For these things, I thank you. Amen.

Notes for Day 8

"God cannot give us a happiness and peace apart from Himself because it is not there. There is no such thing."

C.S. Lewis

Day 9

"The LORD gives me strength. He is like a shield that keeps me safe. My heart trusts in him, and he helps me. My heart jumps for joy. I will sing and give thanks to him."

Psalm 28:7, NIrV

To you I give thanks, My Lord!

You are the strength of my life. I wake up only with your strength. I face the day only with your strength. I take each breath only with your strength. Thank you for holding me up—only with your strength.

You keep me safe, Father. Thank you. You stand before me and confront anything that comes against me; Thank you for being my shield. Thank you for deflecting onslaughts from the enemy.

Thank you for keeping my heart calm when I need help. You help me to think clearly; you stabilize my emotions so they don't run away with me. Thank you that I can tell you anything, and you will not think less of me.

Thank you for not betraying my confidence. I rely on your peace to fill me as I need it.

For these things, I will dance. I will sing and shout of your might. I rejoice in your protection. I twirl in freedom as you fight for me. Bless your name, my Father. Bless you, my God and King.

Morning Thank You:

Mid-Day Thank You:

Evening Thank You:

Bedtime Thank You:

For these things, I thank you. Amen.

Notes for Day 9

"Oh what a happy soul am I although I cannot see. I am resolved that in this world contented I shall be. How many blessings I enjoy that other people don't. To weep and sigh, because I'm blind? I cannot and I won't."

Fanny Crosby

Day 10

"The LORD has been so good to me! How can I ever pay him back?"

Psalm 116:12, NIrV

My Lord,

You alone are my master—the one I serve. No other master compares to you. None is as good as you. Thank you.

My idols turned on me, Lord, but you never change. You are good and will continue to be good now and always. Thank you that I can trust in your goodness. In you, I am secure.

Your generosity overwhelms me. You give good things—things designed especially for me. Your hand overflows with kindness.

Nothing I did in the past earned such goodness for me. Nothing I do in the present and nothing I will ever do in the future can warrant such benefits from you.

Nothing I can do can repay you for your goodness. No amount of money or time can equal your love for me. Even my words and acts of thanksgiving cannot match your demonstrations of love toward me. You have been a feast to me. You have shared your bounty with me, Father. You have shared Jesus.

Morning Thank You:

Mid-Day Thank You:

Evening Thank You:

Bedtime Thank You:

For these things, I thank you. Amen.

Notes for Day 10

"We ought to give thanks for all fortune: if it is good, because it is good; if bad, because it works in us patience, humility, contempt of this world and the hope of our eternal country."

C.S. Lewis

Day 11

"God continues to give us more grace."

James 4:6, NIrV

You amaze me, Father!

Your goodness never stops flowing. Like a river, it makes its way through the rocks of life and the boulders of uncertainty to a waterfall of your love. Thank you for being the source—the spring—of all that's good.

When it seems life is pulling me under and the currents are tossing me from one side to another, you pour out more and more goodness to cushion the blow. You are my life vest, Lord. Thank you.

When I make wrong choices—choices that pull me away from you, God, you show me even more kindness. You draw me to you and remind me You are what I'm looking for: You and nothing—no one—else.

Your goodness and favor are stronger than any storm I face or bring upon myself. Thank you, God. I can't find a love stronger than yours, better than yours, deeper than yours, as infinite as yours.

You give it freely—of your own accord, God. Thank you that I don't need to beg for it. Thank you for all the joys and pleasures of your hand. Thank you for giving of yourself.

Morning Thank You:

Mid-Day Thank You:

Evening Thank You:

Bedtime Thank You:

For these things, I thank you. Amen.

Notes for Day 11

"Be on the lookout for mercies. The more we look for them, the more of them we will see. Blessings brighten when we count them."

Mattie D. Babcock

Day 12

"I thank my God every time I remember you."

Philippians 1:3, NIrV

I remember, Lord!

Thank you for my family, God. I did not choose them; you hand-picked them for me. Thank you, my Father. You knew what I would need and what they would need, and you brought us together for each other. Thank you, that despite family tensions, God, you still work through our relationship problems so your name would be exalted.

My friends, God. What treasures they are to me! You have brought us together; They are my extended family. Thank you for shared interests, for shared beliefs. Thank you that we can accept and celebrate our differences as we show each other the love of God.

My coworkers can be a mixed bag of blessings, Lord. Thank you for each of them: the ones who support me and even the ones who disregard me. God, I thank you that they are helping to grow me into the person you want me to be. Thank you for the conflicts at work that make me rethink my responses to difficult people and situations.

My neighbors. You have placed them in my life for a reason, Lord. Thank you for the opportunities to stop, talk, listen, and share your love with them as I see them entering and leaving their homes.

Morning Thank You:

Mid-Day Thank You:

Evening Thank You:

Bedtime Thank You:

For these things, I thank you. Amen.

Notes for Day 12

"God never promises to remove us from our struggles. He does promise, however, to change the way we look at them."

Max Lucado

Day 13

"So my heart will sing to you. I can't keep silent. Lord, my God, I will give you thanks forever."

Psalm 30:12, NIrV

I will sing, Father!

I will join the grand chorus to praise your name. You give me countless reasons to sing your name, my King. If I had received nothing from your hand, I would nonetheless lift high your name. Jesus, the greatest gift of all! Thank you, my Lord.

My heart swells with emotion, and my heart races within me when I think of your goodness toward me. I can't keep silent, God. The emotions you've given me—the range of them—all feel their fullest when I meditate on your goodness. Awe. Fear. Pride. Humility. My evil. Your love.

Yes, I will sing. I will lift up my voice to the One who inspired heavenly melodies for me—yes, for me. Beloved.

May I abound in song as your love abounds in me. May I make your name known for all you've done for me. May I find every moment to speak of your goodness, to build your name in my world. Not to be silent. Not to be still. To speak. To sing. Your will.

Morning Thank You:

Mid-Day Thank You:

Evening Thank You:

Bedtime Thank You:

For these things, I thank you. Amen.

Notes for Day 13

"Thoughts can be guarded from sin and cultivated to flower with godly joys by remembering that every reflection of our mind and heart is an offering to God of some praise or petition in the voice of his Son."

Bryan Chapell

Day 14

"I have learned to be content no matter what happens to me."

Philippians 4:11, NIrV

Lord, I am learning.

It is difficult, I admit. But thank you for your patience. Thank you for giving me opportunities to learn contentment, Father.

Thank you that it's taking longer than I expect, God. Were I to learn it quickly, I would soon forget. Thank you for these lessons—however difficult they might be.

Thank you for others who have what I've long desired. Thank you for blessing them, for opening your hand of blessings to give them of your bounty.

Thank you for helping me to accept your timing, God. You know all things and know what's best for me. Thank you for your panoramic view.

I depend on you, Father. You will not let me down. I trust you will give me my daily bread, and it will be enough. It is enough, God. You are enough.

Morning Thank You:

Mid-Day Thank You:

Evening Thank You:

Bedtime Thank You:

For these things, I thank you. Amen.

Notes for Day 14

> "Yes, I'm incapable of maintaining an orderly home. Yes, I'm incapable of saving money. Yes, I'm incapable of exercising regularly.... But thanks be to the Super Power [Jesus Christ] who is more than capable!"
>
> Melanie Wilson

Day 15

"He told the crowd to sit down on the ground. He took the seven loaves and gave thanks to God. Then he broke them and gave them to his disciples. They set the loaves down in front of the people. The disciples also had a few small fish. Jesus gave thanks for them too. He told the disciples to pass them around."

Mark 8:6-7, NIrV

Father, you are my provider.

When I've been low on resources—food or fuel—you have made them last longer. You have multiplied my pennies, my few dollars. It's amazing to see how you provide, God. How you've touched others to bring what I need or invite me to share in their blessings. How freely you give! How freely I want to give!

Thank you for trusting me with your fortune, my Lord. Thank you for believing in me to use it for your glory and honor. Thank you for teaching me to manage it in a way that brings honor to you. You give me the wisdom on when, where, and how to manage your estate.

Thank you for the opportunity to bless others with what you've given me. I love to share of your wealth with those around me. Thank you for using me as the vessel to bless others in your name.

Lord, I cherish the opportunity to give back to you a portion of what you've given to me. Thank you for teaching me that everything I own is not truly mine, but yours. Thank you for using the tithe to bless and provide for ministers of your word. Thank you that as I join others in giving back to you, your good news scatters to the ends of earth.

Morning Thank You:

Mid-Day Thank You:

Evening Thank You:

Bedtime Thank You:

For these things, I thank you. Amen.

Notes for Day 15

"If we're in the habit of thanking the Lord in everything, including the painful experiences of life, then the Holy Spirit will fill our hearts with love and praise instead of Satan filling us with bitter venom."

Warren Wiersbe

Day 16

"Keep lies far away from me. Don't make me either poor or rich, but give me only the bread I need each day. If you don't, I might have too much. Then I might say I don't know you. I might say, 'Who is the Lord?' Or I might become poor and steal. Then I would bring shame to the name of my God."

Proverbs 30:8-9, NIrV

My Father,

You know what I need. And I trust you to give it to me—at the right time, at the right place, and in the right way. I leave it all to you, my Lord.

Thank you for being God of my daily bread. Thank you that I have enough because you are more than enough. All I need is you, every day, every moment of the day: You.

Thank you for keeping me honest, my God. Thank you for reminding me to live within my means, to be frugal with what you've given me, to enjoy what I have.

Thank you that I don't have too much; I would have to take care of it all. Thank you for giving me only the things I need to live a life that glorifies you. Thank you for helping me to de-clutter my heart and home from things that pull me away from the most important things.

If I hunger for anything, Lord, let it be more of you. If I am full of anything, my Lord, replace it with more of you. I depend on you.

Morning Thank You:

Mid-Day Thank You:

Evening Thank You:

Bedtime Thank You:

For these things, I thank you. Amen.

Notes for Day 16

"The more we understand God's sovereignty, the more our prayers will be filled with thanksgiving."

R.C. Sproul

Day 17

"But let us give thanks to God! He wins the battle for us because of what our Lord Jesus Christ has done."

1 Corinthians 15:57, NIrV

Father, we're winning!

It doesn't feel like it at times, but I trust: We. Are. Winning.

By others' standards, we might be a few points behind—or not even in the game, but I'm not keeping score, Lord. I know who wins!

Thank you for inviting me onto your team. Thank you for being captain of the team. Thank you for making the wisest choices for the wisest reasons at the wisest times. We. Are. Winning.

Thank you for cheering us on, Holy Spirit. Thank you for encouraging us to keep going, to keep focused, to keep spreading the good news. We. Are. Winning.

Thank you, Jesus, for assuring us the victory. You have conquered death and the grave. It's because of you: We. Are. Winning!

Morning Thank You:

Mid-Day Thank You:

Evening Thank You:

Bedtime Thank You:

For these things, I thank you. Amen.

Notes for Day 17

"Thank God for your forgiveness even when you still feel guilty. Use your guilt feelings as a reminder to give praise to God for His forgiveness."

Erwin Lutzer

Day 18

"Give thanks to God! He always leads us in the winners' parade because we belong to Christ. Through us, God spreads the knowledge of Christ everywhere like perfume."

2 Corinthians 2:14, NIrV

Thank you, God!

I bring to you the highest praise! You are forever before me, Lord. You pave the road; you sweep the debris; you lay the red carpet to victory in Jesus.

My life floats by for all to see—not me, O Lord, but Christ. Your glory. Not my life, my plans, my goals, my story. No, my Lord. Yours, it's your story. Thank you for your story.

For friends and family who cheer me on, thank you, Lord: They're part of Your story. For onlookers wondering how I carry on, thank you, Lord. May they be part of your story. May those who walk quickly by capture the scent of the greatest love story. Jesus Christ! What a story!

Thank you, Father; I am in your story. Thank you for using me to let others know what it's like to know your Son. Thank you for Jesus.

Morning Thank You:

Mid-Day Thank You:

Evening Thank You:

Bedtime Thank You:

For these things, I thank you. Amen.

Dragonflies, Ketchup, and Late-Night Phone Calls

Notes for Day 18

"Worry rarely takes root in a thankful heart."

Randy & Nanci Alcorn

Day 19

"First, I want all of you to pray for everyone. Ask God to bless them. Give thanks for them."

1 Timothy 2:1, NIrV

Thank you, God!

You tell me what you want from me. Thank you, Lord, for the opportunity to lift others up to you in prayer. What a privilege!

It's easy to pray for my loved ones, Lord. Thank you for them, the love we share, and the lessons learned from being in each other's lives. Thank you that we can encourage, support, and motivate each other to walk in your love and freedom every day.

Thank you, God, for those who don't particularly like me and make my life difficult. Thank you that they teach me how to love like you. Bless them, Lord. Bless them, indeed. Thank you for providing for them, for showing them your kindness and love. Thank you for extending mercy to them.

Thank you for those who oppose your Word, Father. It gives me an opportunity to speak more boldly about your love for all men. Thank you for those who question the good news of Jesus Christ and the reality of heaven. They make others think about their final destination and give me the opportunity to share more of your hope.

Morning Thank You:

Mid-Day Thank You:

Evening Thank You:

Bedtime Thank You:

For these things, I thank you. Amen.

Notes for Day 19

"A man in sorrow is in general far nearer God than a man in joy. Gladness may make a man forget his thanksgiving; misery drives him to his prayers."

George MacDonald

Day 20

"I am very pleased with what you have given me. I am very happy with what I've received from you."

Psalm 16:6, NIrV

I am pleased, Lord!

You have chosen for me more than I ever could have imagined. I bow before you, the giver of all things good and perfect.

You delight in hand-selecting my blessings, carefully crafting and designing them just for me. Thank you, my Father! How lovely all that you have given me, how special. How beautiful you are to me.

I am indebted to you for gifts I did not earn or can ever repay. My heart leaps for joy that you would care so much to bless me in ways no one else can. Thank you for the portion assigned to me!

Thank you for things I thought unfair at first—the trials of life, my few possessions. Thank you that you've made them beautiful to me. Thank you for showing me how they glisten through the eyes of thankfulness.

Thank you, my Father, for the heritage inherent in your blessings—the legacy of your faithfulness to my children and grandchildren. I am content with my share in this life. And forever content with my portion in the next.

Morning Thank You:

Mid-Day Thank You:

Evening Thank You:

Bedtime Thank You:

For these things, I thank you. Amen.

Notes for Day 20

"Lord, in Your grace, remind us that You put authorities over us for our protection, and that as we submit to them, we become more like You and experience Your blessing in our lives. Thank you for all the benefits You grant us through submission."

K.P. Yohannan

Day 21

"I will always guide you. I will satisfy your needs in a land that is baked by the sun. I will make you stronger. You will be like a garden that has plenty of water. You will be like a spring whose water never runs dry."

Isaiah 58:11, NIrV

You lead me, Lord!

Forever, you take me by the hand and walk before me. Thank you. I walk safely and securely in your love. Where you go, I go. Where you turn, I turn. Where you stop, I stop. Thank you for being my gentle guide.

You fill me, Father, with your endless cup of comfort. I rely on cool water from your spring of life. Thank you for refreshing me on stress-filled days. Thank you for restoring strength that escapes me in the deserts of life.

Flowers bloom in the garden of my heart, Father. Thank you for new life! Thank you for the hope of your provision, my God, for irrigating my soul with the current of your love.

You are ever-flowing, my Father. You never fail! You are my constant supply; thank you. You watch over me, Lord, and keep me from running dry, from getting parched, from stepping out of your flow.

You are my desire! Thank you for giving me a life full of you.

Morning Thank You:

Mid-Day Thank You:

Evening Thank You:

Bedtime Thank You:

For these things, I thank you. Amen.

Notes for Day 21

"When I think about heaven and pause to thank Jesus for His gift of life, I am always strengthened and refreshed."

Ed Underwood

Day 22

"The Lord is my shepherd. I shall not be in want."

Psalm 23:1, NIV

I want not, Lord!

You are my Master. You ensure I have all I need. You supply all the resources to do your will—to walk in the ways of your love. Thank you!

I stray, my Father, but you know how to bring me back. Thank you! Thank you for knowing that I need to be with you—You and no one and nothing else. Thank you for keeping me close.

You will always be my protector, the one who shields me from attack. I trust you know what is best for me. I trust you know which way is best. I trust you know when it is time to move on or to stay where I am. You know why things happen; I trust you.

Thank you for proving yourself loving. I—a wandering spirit—bow to your faithfulness.

I rest with you on lush, warm grass. I lay at your side. I snuggle at your lap. I fear not. You are here. You remain with me. You are all I need.

Morning Thank You:

Mid-Day Thank You:

Evening Thank You:

Bedtime Thank You:

For these things, I thank you. Amen.

Notes for Day 22

"Thank You that Your love is not dependent on my performance or my physical characteristics."

Cynthia Heald

Day 23

"If we have food and clothing, we will be happy with that."

1 Timothy 6:8, NIrV

Father, I choose happiness!

It might look like my table is bare at times, but you always provide food and fuel for my body. You give me enough—and then some.

I might not have what I want, but I have what I need. Even when I can't see how to combine ingredients into a nourishing meal, you give me inspiration and a love for serving what I have to those I love. Thank you! I am happy with that!

I have shirts, pants, dresses, skirts, and shoes. Thank you. When the sun beats down and beads of sweat form on my skin, I have what I need to keep me cool. When winter blows its freezing temperatures, I have what I need to keep me warm. I am happy with that!

You know what I need; you have reached down and set it on my doorstep. You have sent your angels to distribute food at my door. You have wrapped clothes from others with ribbons of compassion and love. I am happy with that!

Morning Thank You:

Mid-Day Thank You:

Evening Thank You:

Bedtime Thank You:

For these things, I thank you. Amen.

Notes for Day 23

"God is in control, and therefore in everything I can give thanks—not because of the situation but because of the One who directs and rules over it."

Kay Arthur

Day 24

"Having respect for the LORD leads to life. Then you will be content and free from trouble."

Proverbs 19:23, NIrV

I worship you, Lord.

    I come to you with head bowed and heart low. You are the giver of life. You are the source of everything good and perfect. You are the one true God.

    My eyes widen with wonder at the thought of you. How magnificent you are: You know all. You see all. You are all!

    You are the ultimate authority. I yield to your judgment. I yield to your decisions. I yield to your love. In it, I've found life abundant—joy that bubbles up and out of my heart into my world.

    I rest in you, my Lord; I am confident in your sovereignty. Thank you for your comfort; You fill me every day. Thank you for your peace. You give me sleep every night.

I see your touch in the mundane; my heart fills with quiet delight. Suffering stops when I bask in your goodness. Evil stands far away when I revel in you.

I lead a full life. Thank you.

Morning Thank You:

Mid-Day Thank You:

Evening Thank You:

Bedtime Thank You:

For these things, I thank you. Amen.

Notes for Day 24

"The art of being happy lies in the power of extracting happiness from common things."

Henry Ward Beecher

Day 25

"The living creatures give glory, honor and thanks to the One who sits on the throne and who lives for ever and ever."

Revelation 4:9, NIrV

I give you glory, Lord!

Every living creature praises you. They utter and sing and roar your name. From north to south, from east to west, creation rises in applause of you.

You are due the praise, Magnificent One. You are due the symphony of your handiwork. You are due the chorus of your saints.

The first of your creation blesses your name. We—the last—of your creation too. The works of your hands—the tiniest of yet undiscovered life—speak of your might.

I thank you, O Lord, for surrounding me with your art. You who sit on high—so far and yet so near—burst with grandeur and majesty.

Praise your name, O God! Praise your name, King of Kings! Praise your name, Almighty One! Praise your name, Divine Creator!

None lives forever! None but Jehovah!

Morning Thank You:

Mid-Day Thank You:

Evening Thank You:

Bedtime Thank You:

For these things, I thank you. Amen.

Notes for Day 25

"Everything has its wonders, even darkness and silence, and I learn, whatever state I may be in, therein to be content."

Helen Keller

Day 26

*"Let them give thanks to the LORD for his faithful love.
Let them give thanks for the miracles he does for his
people. Let them sacrifice thank offerings. Let them talk
about what he has done as they sing with joy."*

Psalm 107:21-22, NIrV

Praise to the Lord!

Accept my praise, my Lord! I place it on your altar—my offering to you alone. I drape myself on the table of your holiness; I present myself to you.

I have seen your miracles—the wonders of your hand. I marvel at the supremacy of your name. None other compares to you, Jesus! You are great.

Displays of your love are too numerous for me. So frequent, so lavish, so pure. I tell—no, I sing—of what you have done, my ringing praise to you.

No strings attach themselves to your love. No limits restrict the range of it. Your love sees no horizon. It has no beginning or end. Thank you for your infinite love.

I, your child, celebrate you; I acknowledge your name. I give news of your works; I fill my log with your deeds.

Love marches by in procession—a parade from you to me.

Morning Thank You:

Mid-Day Thank You:

Evening Thank You:

Bedtime Thank You:

For these things, I thank you. Amen.

Notes for Day 26

"God is most glorified in us when we are most satisfied in Him."

John Piper

Day 27

"They said, 'Lord God who rules over all, we give thanks to you. You are the One who is and who was. We give you thanks because you have taken your great power and have begun to rule.'"

Revelation 11:17, NIrV

You rule, Lord!

You are King of Kings. I call out to you: Reign! Reign over me, reign over my world, reign over every living thing and every situation.

Thank you that you're in charge—and not me. Thank you for controlling all. I can't. Thank you for being eternal. Never-ending. Timeless. Immortal. The one true God has forever existed and forever will be. Praise to you!

Your kingdom expands beyond galaxies—beyond worlds we've never known. Arise from your throne, O King. Spread your arms out in dominion. Reign! Reign over all, Lord!

You alone know justice. You alone know mercy. You use one alongside the other. You, O Lord, reign in love.

Thank you for your mighty and merciful hand. Thank you for your strength and compassion. Thank you for your kingly power. Thank you for your love.

Morning Thank You:

Mid-Day Thank You:

Evening Thank You:

Bedtime Thank You:

For these things, I thank you. Amen.

Notes for Day 27

"Contentment with the divine will is the best remedy we can apply to misfortunes."

William Temple

Day 28

"I will give thanks to the LORD because he does what is right. I will sing praise to the LORD Most High."

Psalm 7:17, NIrV

You do what is right, Lord!

    Thank you for righting wrongs. Thank you for standing tall. Thank you for defending me. "This is my child!"

    I trust your judgment. I trust your process. You know when to step in. You say, "It is time." Thank you!

    You do not waver, my Father. You do not hesitate. You are forever just, forever honorable, forever true.

    You check the balances; you verify the weights. You proclaim justice; you decide. Thank you!

I give you due praise; I'm singing your name. Jesus, most high. Jesus, divine. Jesus, my advocate. My king. You. Are. Right.

Morning Thank You:

Mid-Day Thank You:

Evening Thank You:

Bedtime Thank You:

For these things, I thank you. Amen.

Notes for Day 28

"This is the secret of being content: To learn and accept that we live daily by God's unmerited favor given through Christ, and that we can respond to any and every situation by His divine enablement through the Holy Spirit."

Jerry Bridges

Day 29

"Let Christ's word live in you like a rich treasure. Teach and correct each other wisely. Sing psalms, hymns and spiritual songs. Sing with thanks in your hearts to God."

Colossians 3:16, NIrV

Thank you for living in me, O Lord!

My heart is your address—the place you chose to dwell. You knocked at my door; I welcomed you in. You unpacked your love and stayed with me. Thank you!

You reign, O God! Thank you for moving in every room of my life, in every corner of my house. Thank you for spreading the aroma of your love for all who dwell with me and all who enter. Thank you, dear King.

You brought me your word, now my most valued possession. A precious stone, a gem. Jesus Christ, my rock. Thank you for correcting, teaching, and guiding me through your Word.

Your Word disrobes your love for me, Jesus in flesh for all to see. The word of life hung on the cross, all he lost for me.

Your love is my anthem, my sacred song to you. Most Holy One, my audience. My Master, I sing for you.

Morning Thank You:

Mid-Day Thank You:

Evening Thank You:

Bedtime Thank You:

For these things, I thank you. Amen.

Dragonflies, Ketchup, and Late-Night Phone Calls

Notes for Day 29

"Never say there is nothing beautiful in the world anymore. There is always something to make you wonder in the shape of a tree, the trembling of a leaf."

Albert Schweitzer

Day 30

"You will be made rich in every way. Then you can always give freely. We will take your many gifts to the people who need them. And they will give thanks to God."

2 Corinthians 9:11, NIrV

I am rich, my Lord!

I overflow with the wealth of your love and goodness. Thank you for your gifts, the displays of your affection, your delight in me. Thank you for spreading them out before me, for wrapping them with care with the ribbons of your extravagance. I am rich, my Lord!

Wealth comes from no one else. You own all, you control all, you distribute all. You give freely; your hand is open. Always extended, always expanding, always welcoming.

Thank you for your gifts, my God—gifts of love, gifts of plenty, gifts of sacrifice. Never closed, never stingy, never grumbling or complaining. You are my example. You are my model. You and you alone. Thank you.

Thank you for those who need. Thank you: They will receive. Gifts from me, gifts from you, gifts from eternity.

Morning Thank You:

Mid-Day Thank You:

Evening Thank You:

Bedtime Thank You:

For these things, I thank you. Amen.

Notes for Day 30

"Whenever you get a blessing from God, give it back to Him as a love gift.... If you hoard a thing for yourself, it will turn into spiritual dry rot, as the manna did when it was hoarded. God will never let you hold a spiritual thing for yourself; it has to be given back to Him that He may make it a blessing to others."

Oswald Chambers

Day 31

"I will satisfy the priests. I will give them more than enough. And my people will be filled with the good things I give them,' announces the Lord."

Jeremiah 31:14 NIrV

You declare it, Lord!

You will satisfy me. You will fill my cup. You will immerse and saturate me in your love.

I, a member of your royal family, the one you have adopted as your own, will overflow with your blessings. Thank you for your abundant love!

Thank you for showers of blessings. Thank you for supplying me with the best crops from your bounty. Thank you for feasts from your table. Everything that comes from your hand is good. You are good.

I have little space left in my heart and home for more of your goodness. Yet you keep giving. You keep pouring. You keep presenting me with your best. Thank you.

What you announce you will do, O King. You are faithful. You are true. You are amen.

Thank you.

Morning Thank You:

Mid-Day Thank You:

Evening Thank You:

Bedtime Thank You:

For these things, I thank you. Amen.

Notes for Day 31

"Jesus is moved to happiness every time He sees that you appreciate what He has done for you. Grip His pierced hand and say to Him, 'I thank Thee, Saviour, because Thou has died for me.' Thank Him likewise for all the other blessings He has showered upon you from day to day. It brings joy to Jesus."

Ole Hallesby

Thank You

How did it go?

I trust *Dragonflies, Ketchup, and Late-Night Phone Calls* encouraged you just as much as it encouraged me when I was writing it. The journal truly has helped me remain thankful every day, throughout the day.

If *Dragonflies, Ketchup, and Late-Night Phone Calls* has helped you, would you send me your feedback? Would you let me know the great things God has done with you through this book?

Also, I would be thankful if you gave me a five-star rating and a glowing review on Amazon or GoodReads.

Who knows? You just might be included as one of my specific blessings to God in one of my very own journal entries.

List of Bible Verses Used

"They stood every morning to thank and praise the Lord. They did the same thing every evening."

1 Chronicles 23:30 NIrV

"Give thanks no matter what happens. God wants you to thank him because you believe in Christ Jesus."

1 Thessalonians 5:18, NIrV

"Give thanks to the Lord, because he is good. His faithful love continues forever."

Psalm 107:1, NIrV

"Thanks be to God for his indescribable gift!"

2 Corinthians 9:15, NIV

"Give thanks to the LORD, call on his name; make known among the nations what he has done."

Psalm 105:1, NIV

"Spend a lot of time in prayer. Always be watchful and thankful."

Colossians 4:2, NIrV

"Do everything you say or do in the name of the Lord Jesus. Always give thanks to God the Father through Christ."

Colossians 3:17, NIrV

"Give thanks as you enter the gates of his temple. Give praise as you enter its courtyards. Give thanks to him and praise his name."

Psalm 100:4, NIrV

"You and your families will eat at the place the LORD your God will choose. He will be with you there. You will find joy in everything you have done. That's because he has blessed you."

Deuteronomy 12:7, NIrV

"The LORD gives me strength. He is like a shield that keeps me safe. My heart trusts in him, and he helps me. My heart jumps for joy. I will sing and give thanks to him."

Psalm 28:7, NIrV

"The LORD has been so good to me! How can I ever pay him back?"

Psalm 116:12, NIrV

"God continues to give us more grace."

James 4:6, NIrV

"I thank my God every time I remember you."

Philippians 1:3, NIrV

"So my heart will sing to you. I can't keep silent. Lord, my God, I will give you thanks forever."

Psalm 30:12, NIrV

"I have learned to be content no matter what happens to me."

Philippians 4:11, NIrV

"He told the crowd to sit down on the ground. He took the seven loaves and gave thanks to God. Then he broke them and gave them to his disciples. They set the loaves down in front of the people. The disciples also had a few small fish. Jesus gave thanks for them too. He told the disciples to pass them around."

Mark 8:6-7, NIrV

"But let us give thanks to God! He wins the battle for us because of what our Lord Jesus Christ has done."

1 Corinthians 15:57, NIrV

"Keep lies far away from me. Don't make me either poor or rich, but give me only the bread I need each day. If you don't, I might have too much. Then I might say I don't know you. I might say, 'Who is the Lord?' Or I might become poor and steal. Then I would bring shame to the name of my God."

Proverbs 30:8-9, NIrV

"Give thanks to God! He always leads us in the winners' parade because we belong to Christ. Through us, God spreads the knowledge of Christ everywhere like perfume."

2 Corinthians 2:14, NIrV

"First, I want all of you to pray for everyone. Ask God to bless them. Give thanks for them."

1 Timothy 2:1, NIrV

> "I am very pleased with what you have given me. I am very happy with what I've received from you."
>
> Psalm 16:6, NIrV

> "I will always guide you. I will satisfy your needs in a land that is baked by the sun. I will make you stronger. You will be like a garden that has plenty of water. You will be like a spring whose water never runs dry."
>
> Isaiah 58:11, NIrV

> "The Lord is my shepherd. I shall not be in want."
>
> Psalm 23:1, NIV

> "If we have food and clothing, we will be happy with that."
>
> 1 Timothy 6:8, NIrV

"Having respect for the LORD leads to life. Then you will be content and free from trouble."

Proverbs 19:23, NIrV

"The living creatures give glory, honor and thanks to the One who sits on the throne and who lives for ever and ever."

Revelation 4:9, NIrV

"Let them give thanks to the LORD for his faithful love. Let them give thanks for the miracles he does for his people. Let them sacrifice thank offerings. Let them talk about what he has done as they sing with joy."

Psalm 107:21-22, NIrV

"They said, 'Lord God who rules over all, we give thanks to you. You are the One who is and who was. We give you thanks because you have taken your great power and have begun to rule.'"

Revelation 11:17, NIrV

"I will give thanks to the LORD because he does what is right. I will sing praise to the LORD Most High."

Psalm 7:17, NIrV

"Let Christ's word live in you like a rich treasure. Teach and correct each other wisely. Sing psalms, hymns and spiritual songs. Sing with thanks in your hearts to God."

Colossians 3:16, NIrV

"You will be made rich in every way. Then you can always give freely. We will take your many gifts to the people who need them. And they will give thanks to God."

2 Corinthians 9:11, NIrV

"'I will satisfy the priests. I will give them more than enough. And my people will be filled with the good things I give them,' announces the Lord."

Jeremiah 31:14 NIrV

List of Quotes Used

"Perhaps it takes a purer faith to praise God for unrealized blessings than for those we once enjoyed or those we enjoy now."

A.W. Tozer

"We pray for the big things and forget to give thanks for the ordinary, small (and yet really not small) gifts."

Dietrich Bonhoeffer

"Here are the two best prayers I know: 'Help me, help me, help me' and 'Thank you, thank you, thank you.'"

Anne Lamott

"There is a way to live the big of giving thanks in all things. It is this: to give thanks in this one small thing. The moments will add up."

Ann Voskamp

"A state of mind that sees God in everything is evidence of growth in grace and a thankful heart."

Charles Finney

"God is pleased with no music below so much as with the thanksgiving songs of relieved widows and supported orphans; of rejoicing, comforted, and thankful persons."

Jeremy Taylor

"Yes, give thanks for 'all things' for, as it has been well said 'Our disappointments are but His appointments.'"

A.W. Pink

"God cannot give us a happiness and peace apart from Himself because it is not there. There is no such thing."

C.S. Lewis

"Oh what a happy soul am I although I cannot see, I am resolved that in this world contented I shall be. How many blessings I enjoy that other people don't. To weep and sigh, because I'm blind? I cannot and I won't."

Fanny Crosby

"We ought to give thanks for all fortune: if it is good, because it is good; if bad, because it works in us patience, humility, contempt of this world and the hope of our eternal country."

C.S. Lewis

"Be on the lookout for mercies. The more we look for them, the more of them we will see. Blessings brighten when we count them."

Mattie D. Babcock

"God never promises to remove us from our struggles. He does promise, however, to change the way we look at them."

Max Lucado

"Thoughts can be guarded from sin and cultivated to flower with godly joys by remembering that every reflection of our mind and heart is an offering to God of some praise or petition in the voice of his Son."

Bryan Chapell

"Yes, I'm incapable of maintaining an orderly home. Yes, I'm incapable of saving money. Yes, I'm incapable of exercising regularly.... But thanks be to the Super Power [Jesus Christ] who is more than capable!"

Melanie Wilson

"If we're in the habit of thanking the Lord in everything, including the painful experiences of life, then the Holy Spirit will fill our hearts with love and praise instead of Satan filling us with bitter venom."

Warren Wiersbe

"The more we understand God's sovereignty, the more our prayers will be filled with thanksgiving."

R.C. Sproul

"Thank God for your forgiveness even when you still feel guilty. Use your guilt feelings as a reminder to give praise to God for His forgiveness."

Erwin Lutzer

"Worry rarely takes root in a thankful heart."

Randy & Nanci Alcorn

"A man in sorrow is in general far nearer God than a man in joy. Gladness may make a man forget his thanksgiving; misery drives him to his prayers."

George MacDonald

"Lord, in Your grace, remind us that You put authorities over us for our protection, and that as we submit to them, we become more like You and experience Your blessing in our lives. Thank you for all the benefits You grant us through submission."

K.P. Yohannan

"When I think about heaven and pause to thank Jesus for His gift of life, I am always strengthened and refreshed."

Ed Underwood

"Thank You that Your love is not dependent on my performance or my physical characteristics."

Cynthia Heald

"God is in control, and therefore in everything I can give thanks—not because of the situation but because of the One who directs and rules over it."

Kay Arthur

"The art of being happy lies in the power of extracting happiness from common things."

Henry Ward Beecher

"Everything has its wonders, even darkness and silence, and I learn, whatever state I may be in, therein to be content."

Helen Keller

"God is most glorified in us when we are most satisfied in Him."

John Piper

"Contentment with the divine will is the best remedy we can apply to misfortunes."

William Temple

"This is the secret of being content: To learn and accept that we live daily by God's unmerited favor given through Christ, and that we can respond to any and every situation by His divine enablement through the Holy Spirit."

Jerry Bridges

"Never say there is nothing beautiful in the world anymore. There is always something to make you wonder in the shape of a tree, the trembling of a leaf."

Albert Schweitzer

"Whenever you get a blessing from God, give it back to Him as a love gift.... If you hoard a thing for yourself, it will turn into spiritual dry rot, as the manna did when it was hoarded. God will never let you hold a spiritual thing for yourself; it has to be given back to Him that He may make it a blessing to others."

Oswald Chambers

"Jesus is moved to happiness every time He sees that you appreciate what He has done for you. Grip His pierced hand and say to Him, 'I thank Thee, Saviour, because Thou has died for me.' Thank Him likewise for all the other blessings He has showered upon you from day to day. It brings joy to Jesus."

Ole Hallesby

About Daphne

Daphne Tarango is a freelance writer who comforts hurting women with the comfort she has received from God. Daphne inspires women to take biblical steps to personal growth and freedom. She also writes about her struggles with chronic illness and pain.

Daphne's work has appeared in *Just Between Us*, *{in}courage* (a division of DaySpring), *Living Better 50+*, *The Gabriel*, *Inspired Women Magazine*, *Ruby for Women*, *Rest Ministries*, and *Mentoring Moments for Christian Women*. Daphne contributed three chapters in the compilation *Women of the Secret Place* (Ambassador International, 2012). The thankfulness journal, *Dragonflies, Ketchup, and Late-Night Phone Calls*, is her first book.

Daphne speaks at recovery events. She was a leader in a local Christ-centered recovery program, where she facilitated open-share and step study groups.

Daphne lives in the Southeastern United States. She retired from corporate life at a Fortune 500 company to become a stay-at-home mom. She is the President of Lakeland Christian Writers, a chapter of American Christian Writers (ACW).

Daphne enjoys solitude; nature walks; journaling; experimenting in the kitchen; the arts; and spending time with her newlywed husband, her three children, their basset hound Dudleigh, and ornery Kitty-Kitty too.

Connect with Daphne

To connect with Daphne, email
daphnetarango@gmail.com.

Or visit one of the following:

Facebook

DaphneWrites-Comfort for the Journey

LinkedIn

Daphne Tarango

Twitter

@Daphne_Writes

Made in United States
Orlando, FL
27 December 2025